It Seems Like a Mighty Long time

Also by Angela Jackson

Dark Legs and Silk Kisses: The Beatitudes of the Spinners

And All These Roads Be Luminous

Where I Must Go: A Novel

It Seems Like a Mighty Long time

POEMS

Angela Jackson

TRIQUARTERLY BOOKS / NORTHWESTERN UNIVERSITY PRESS

EVANSTON, ILLINOIS

Northwestern University Press
www.nupress.northwestern.edu

Copyright © 2015 by Angela Jackson. Published 2015 by TriQuarterly Books/Northwestern
University Press. All rights reserved.

Printed in the United States of America

10 9 8 7 6 5 4 3 2 1

Library of Congress Cataloging-in-Publication Data
Jackson, Angela, 1951– author.
    It seems like a mighty long time : poems / Angela Jackson.
       pages cm
    ISBN 978-0-8101-3051-7 (pbk. : alk. paper) — ISBN 978-0-8101-6817-6 (ebook)
    I. Title.
    PS3560.A179I86 2015
    811.54—dc23

                                                                          2014033228

The paper used in this publication meets the minimum requirements of the American National
Standard for Information Sciences—Permanence of Paper for Printed Library Materials, ANSI
Z39.48-1992.

For the Ones Who Really Love Me

For All the Years

For Mama

For Debra Anne Jackson

1958–2008

CONTENTS

III

IV. Suite: Ida

V

VI

VII

VIII

***

ACKNOWLEDGMENTS

This book has benefited from the support of many people. I have many people to thank. These include:

Parneshia Jones, poetry editor, for her patience and expertise.

Anne Gendler for her precise care.

Reginald Gibbons, Cornelia Spelman, and Carole A. Parks for their wise advice on the shaping of this book.

Major Jackson for his expert advice on the revision of several of these poems.

Rudy E. Faust for excellent publicity.

Gianna Mosser for extensive back work.

Roella C. Davis for technical support and invaluable aid.

Naeem Jackson and Matthew Jackson for necessary technical assistance.

Marianne Jankowski for the lovely cover and Jonathan Green for permission to use his stunning painting.

Thanks and Praise.

Some of the poems from this volume were previously published in *Black Renaissance Noire, Black Scholar, Callaloo, Emergence, Expressions from Englewood, Lyric, Mourning Katrina, Reverie,* and *TriQuarterly Online.* My gratitude to the editors of those publications.

It Seems Like a Mighty Long Time

Mississippi Summer

I never heard her say "catfish ministrate"
Like women. If I had I would have stopped
My own blood that had begun just before
I came to Brown's Addition, in the Queen
City of the Delta, believing if I ran
Fast enough, womanhood would not
Catch me. I was not "smart." I did not
Hurry to do chores, but rushed to explore
The beauties of the place where I was born,
First saw daylight. I longed for it, before
I left it, as I breathed in deeply the fog
That killed malarial mosquitoes that trailed
The truck that took up most of the road
I walked in sandals till my feet were dirty
As Mary Magdalene who followed Him
As I swore I would the rest of my natural
Life and after. But I do not remember
Seeing the inside of a church the whole
Time I was in the midst of old women
Who slept with Bibles but could not read
Them. X marks the spot my grandmother
Signed her name, where she drowned in sun-
Light as she suffered the headaches that wove her
Through the house but did not stop her. Was it
Her blood, rushing to her head, instead of
Between her legs where fifteen
Children had pushed out and took what

Life had for them and hard scrambled
For the rest? Her husband, a tough lesson
To teach, lived around the corner in a tiny
Room-house, leaned on his cane, shooed
Greedy birds away from his tiny pears.
Smiling like a dream-drunk who came
To visit. Hard to believe he was my father's
Father. His rough edges worn smooth by
Time like a jagged stone smooth as a marble
Or pearl so tiny you could hold it in the palm of
Your hand. There was no water in him.
You had to be a certain kind of man to keep
So many children alive near Keep-A-Running,
Mississippi. Blossoms—pink, red, white—I blew my way
Through them like a breeze, no one could catch,
But Cooda could outrun me. I did my best
Even at play. Wise enough to know I would
Be remembered as my mother's child, my father's
Child by old women and men who pinned a piece
Of their hopes on me. Whether they wanted to or not.

\

Know that love has chosen you . . .
—ROBERT HAYDEN

the Fabric of Our Lives

The streets had a cushion then
                      like velvet.
And streetlights shone like satin.

The wind gave us lashes
           our parents wore
                  on their backs.

Mothers, fathers made velvet; saw by satin
sounds of dreamers. Medium brown
in touch with spirits, rejected
just enough to be tough
Enough to be proud.

Everyone remembered cotton, the bolls of it,
their backs still holding the bow,
arms, hands still holding the pick,
the toil of it.
Our cushioned streets
so many beats from cotton.

Wearing the wind's warp and woof.
The trees so bright, each leaf
a sequin.

Crowning

I was crowning marble-Mary with bright
colored flowers. I, in pastel silk,
quiet, closed as a girl-queen, not light
as those girls like butter, milk.

He worked three-leven, the post office,
from lifting sacks, to punching in zip codes.
She cooked, scrubbed, till she felt it in her wrist.
Did it for us to walk new aisles, roads.

Me, among rows and rows of brown-black grads
in full white wedding dresses, so white they
shine in a church of arches, sublime, sad
windows that tell each of us to pray.

I walk the aisle this day and memory.
Flowers, now, for the ones who really love me.

Perfect Pears

My father nibbled our cheeks
like a king nibbling pears, one at a time,
holding each perfectly still. Our mouths shaped O
in infant ecstasy.

A love so fierce and tender!

His mustache brushed like livid breath
upon our new skin. We loved that too.

He turned his right leg into a horse
and let us ride, bumping along through
a safe life.

At the post office, a king among men,
carrying the heavy sacks of letters, swollen
urgent shapes, did he dream of the hard
pears in his father's yard on that tree
pears turned ripe and sweet?

Later, what an imperfect king, prone
to temper, he whipped us into lineage.
Tolerating nothing he deemed outside
the rule of his kingdom.

A love so fierce and fearsome!

Like any king he offered us protection.
We were arrogant beggars who accepted
his food, his shelter, and conspired
against him in whispers, until we
at distance learned to love him like pears
once again.

Now my sister has a pear tree in her front yard.
Pears rain down onto her porch, bruise and bleed
on concrete, or gray squirrely squirrels high in branches
cast down pears they've ruined
with their mean teeth.

My Father's Prayers

Every morning my father prayed on his knees
at the side of his marriage bed. He bowed
his head and poured his prayers into two loose fists
over his mouth. We watched in wonder
as the one who could give a whipping
and scald us with his tongue turned
into a penitent child; obedient and
intense, petitioner. We lurked around his doorway
like cowardly debtors observing his
rich rite of passage into the working day
or weekend that worked also, except
for Sunday when he got up, dressed
in his best, put on his hat and went
calling on relatives, our Aunt Tumpy
who had a piano. He could make it
talk; the keys jangling an entrance
to Paradise. Blue fire in his fingers. He threw his head back
and let his hands go with his relaxed, ecstatic body.
And with each sound he threw away or burned
away everything that hurt a man or
brought him to his knees.

territory

I rouse her and she looks at the clock.
I could not sleep in the noisy dark. We dress.
We go down to the basement together.
It is the hour between midnight and one
o'clock. Upstairs the radiators are singing, raw
without lubricant, grinding without protection.
My mother turns the key
in the padlock.
I hold the light, a circle around her.

We enter,
walk over the wet, concrete floors.
My mother holds the tiny oil can.
I hold the heavy light.
She squeezes oil into the furnace pipe;
the place where oil goes
she knows.
The basement was my father's
territory.

Behind us is a dark, grimy counter where he worked.
He knew what he was doing
and he did it
alone.

In the darkness I see him, ghost-light, moving, working
at his workbench. His shoulders a study of what it means
to hold together a house with wife and children inside.

In the darkness he is a youngish man, then old,
holding together promises made in centuries of unremunerated toil,
in the hustle and rustle of the city.
His is uncharted territory to me. The masculine wonder
and defeat. The victory.
Now, after midnight,
the loneliness of this territory
cries out to us.
We hurry back up the stairs.
Stumbling through the light.

Hope

My mother could not understand how it happened
That her brother's son died in his car on the railroad tracks
When it was struck by a train.
She could not understand that grim bewitching hope
That clung to the tips of his fingers stubborn as calluses
As he turned the key in the ignition.
The motor turned over and went back to sleep like a grouchy husband
Who will not listen when the wife shakes him awake
Because the house is on fire; the engine died
In its sleep,
They were dreaming then, my cousin and his friend,
Of a grand escape with the hot breath of the train on the side
Of their fear sweaty faces (steel had never split ribs and splashed blood
Past split skin, and their skulls had not been left crushed and leaking).
They were dreaming of being old men in slippers
Telling the story of how they got away just
In time.

Mama in Blue, White, and Love

Was this in your blue
print? That I be tempted by blue
devils to cry instead of laugh thunderously?
Is this the song (not blues)
you planned for me?
When did you map it out meticulously
in the midnight
house in a country of white as dead bones
laws that would have struck you blind
instead of right to witness winning blue sky
horizons blue-penciled
for your honest dream
for me? You kept dreaming.
Do you recall how white
people could do anything
to people of our hue or genes?
Once your family fled north
to avoid the twisted gray rope.
Were you working on the print for me
then when you returned?
Or were you born with it as a fingerprint?
Or a footnote?

Did you walk your map for me
and daughters in blue
stockings and uniforms
or bare legs who write with soft
palms what you wrote with hard
caress and powerful grip against hot

trouble, hot blue
water in a tub in an open
yard in a closed land.
The parts of your life I cannot
consider, did you?
The short order courses of the hotel kitchen
where your coworker spit
in nasty whites' food,
did you serve the blue
plate special?
Weren't you special
who brought everything good you could
home to us? Did you draw a daughter in blue
jeans off to a wide dream amid blue
books, African-American blue
blood with no register beyond the reckoning
of my life and yours?
Was I in your blue
print: a blues
note amid blue
racers weaving? Is it once in a blue
moon I kiss your blue
collar and pin your blue
ribbon in your gray-white hair?

In My Father's House Are Many Stories

For George "Sunni Man" Jackson, 1921–1993

My father made a garden by an expressway; the topsoil was grime, and neglected foot steps. My mother could not wash the exhausted soil from her windows for longer than the time it took her hands to heal from the hot vinegar solution. (They did not quit bending this mother, this father, bending from deep in the back. They did not quit straightening things contrived in crookedness.)

Every day is a form of trying. Every day in my memory is a gesture beyond acquiescence, though the whole city, the weight of it, suffocated and stunted portions of the self, clipped the wings of the dance, garbled some poem. I do not remember the blues as simple defeat. Every time I open my mouth is a form of trying.

If all word of me be used up and lost like newspapers rolling over and over on the way to the blind slam against a building, all my rolling a gesture beyond acquiescence. The earth will love me. Or I will wiggle through the cracks contrived to break my mother's back and I will blossom in the memory of footsteps in the way they did not quit.

My father returned to Mississippi to build a second story to the single story frame house where I was born after five others. He made space for daughters and sons of daughters, safe under one roof definite as blues sky he would lift into place with his hands that trembled a little with agitations sometimes when he could not call a piece of memory or story as fast as once.

He lifted that house on blocks and opened the roof to a wide dream too unfinished for him to stay inside. He moved around his mother's house amid dust and mice, to feast on dreams prepared in the monotony of the post office factory he hates to the death of every day. He nods to the boarded mouth of his father's house, to the pear tree, to the pecan, to the torn swing swaying air, no body cooling on the cooling boards. No story waiting for audience there.

Once, come Chicago-home from Home, he stood in the kitchen doorway, frightened still by the shining ghost who stood at the foot of his mother's high bed, speechless, both of them ghost and fleshed-out ghost, my father, nervous and certain of the visitation Mama disputed with reason crafted to quell his excitement. The northern sun crowded us together into the kitchen of that yellow frame house. My father's memory grew wider, open to fancies, fluencies.

Remember Germany. Where women and children called him "swartze" and king. Benevolent despot of nylons and candies. All the hero he ever was crooning out and in through black skin, turned barbed wire like the fences across the river where American Japanese waited in embrace throughout the war. Swartze king came home to barbed wire. He remembers Germany.

Once as a boy riding with Uncle Sweet in their father's wagon, a star fell down in a field near the road and lit the earth, earth opened up, brightness blossoming to near blindness. His Papa stopped the wagon and waited for some word to call this wonder to pass between them. But everywhere was mean, so he hid this in some narrow corridor to the great chambers he would only learn to live in a song, momentary and wry.

A thousand-fold the shame-story told over and again disguised as trickery in my father's eye. Triumph told and told lest shame sit in his mouth, and rot his teeth, and sink his cheeks, and his face be skull. All those mouths to feed. And the mouth of a dream yawning like an emperor bored with the pain of the peasant. The be-ringed hand across the mouth of a city, a country that called him nigger and worse while he denied degradation. And we children sang our songs into fans of summer that flew back song like amplified angels, death-defying because he and she made it so. A long window to shout out to the streets of the naked emperor who would not remember our names.

We grew swift on his anger, my father deposed and eloquent. We learned flight and early reply graceful as the path of stars rising out of the earth in a twist of his grand memory.

This is the second story of my father's house.

Children, hewn from wood of the tree he tells about that waters itself. That story. Blues songs and lost harmonicas, house shoes we bought he would not wear. Walking on the sides of his feet tracing the shape of his mother's grave and the edge of his own in hers.

Stories told a thousand times. And wife as sharp angel had heard all the telling. Stories. Not enough building to hold all the children inside.

In his century-lived, gone mother's house did he see at night in the tree-thick dark a leaf of light at the foot of the bed? Did it rattle and reach to speak? What did he reply? What did he say as a boy when the star-swallowing earth grew a coat of bright color that blazed and blazes this moment he will not lose? And the story of his destiny is written more quietly than he wanted in this moment and that when the earth itself opened and light came out the center of the dark to meet the light that tumbled from sky giving my father voice for dream I give back to him now. His story amplified by a gift of tongues. A house sheltering wonder and shame.

House with sunroof, skylight, windows, and tree that waters itself inside the great and listening chambers where begins the beat of a blues he gave himself to singing on a cruise on the Mississippi River. That house solid, constructed of deliberate hands and intelligent will, many roomed, stories, blues he lives inside and beyond beyond oh, beyond acquiescence.

‖

Who is that bird
reporting the storm?
—GWENDOLYN BROOKS

Elam House

Hair brushed and bound. They
Sat up all night on the train.
Traveling between the wing of a Crow
And the sleeves of a moon white
As latrines in the South they were
Denied.

Their shoes tied to calves, the laced legs
Hidden. They longed to help rouged
Pink ladies enough to send money home.
And live at Elam on their own—
Sunday tea and gentlemen callers.

After Elam, freedom, wedlock or not.
But what husband could save a woman
From a crow's wing of the South
Or crow's feet anywhere?
Or the moon's sleeves with anything
Up them to ruin girl's reputation
Or send her high on the rustle of doves?
Or shine on a bed in which she must lie
Listening to the grinding of teeth
Wondering: Is it me? Will I be happy
By and by?

She'd make her bed hard
And turn over often.
And he'd turn over with her.

And what was hard was hot.
If she had to burn for all her mistakes,
Why not then, with him,
This way?

If anyone smelled her burning
They could bring cold water.
Not a glass, but a bowl of porcelain
Perfect as the ubiquitous northern moon.

the Day after All Saints Day Is All Souls Day

Because we have to wander in dark fitted skin
Through years folded in thousands like exotic, embroidered fans
Until we find ourselves, and then
The light to go in

To a shimmering atop a well out of which the light
Leaks in earthly shape. We dream and cheat
A peek at an Eden or a Paradise,
The sight of light itself undressing in the evening
Where the dark that we are reaches out
For everything

We have missed the chance to be saints
Right away. Did not wear long white dresses stiff
With argo starch or severe black suits;
Did not beat the tambourine, shout, or dance in ecstasy,
Did not sweep the air with flat funeral parlor fans
On any day of the week.

We were too much of the world—
Watched soaps, smoked cigarettes, drank an occasional
White wine, listened to our sex drives, rode
Them—
   Suffered to be purified, but not enough to be wise.

Her Memory Coming Home

Her mouth is open. But she's not
Singing. Her eyes are closed.
But she's not sleep. A rest-pause at eleven o'clock
While the wheels of the church bus
Take her from singing to distress.

Fifteen years ago she was in love,
A knot of time. It
Didn't work out.
He never laid a hand on her that wasn't
Like a wing in flight.
She flew under him.

He came into a room and made the furniture
Make sense.
Stretched out on the sofa.
Put his coffee feet on the coffee table.
The bed he made a sea.
He made a sky at eleven
                An hour before midnight.

Love is a strange dish.
Some people only try it once.
Sometimes it's only served
One time. Plates go right past you.

Her mouth water—
A singing. Her eyes are closed.
Oh, God is good—God made everything
—sea, coffee, wing, knot, sky.
                    Dish, eleven o'clock.
Curious. Belief doesn't diminish desire.
The eyes flutter, fly open.

Photograph: Circa 1960

How wide the sidewalks were!
You stood in the middle of ours.
Definite and debonair.

Mama with a big black
Patent leather handbag.
Strap
Draped over her arm.
Chic. Loose coat holding no baby inside.

Madaddy suited, slanted wide brim hat.
At attention
As if he were seeing Paris
After the war.

All smiles.

Behind them the tall trees
Made shade. And fences
Held back the houses
And kept them off the sidewalk
And out of the street
Steel-veined with streetcar lines
Before they were erased like markings
From a game of hopscotch.

Were there shadows rolling in under the trees?
I see them now.

A thousand pages

(After the documentary, 2007)

When they came for him they came
with flashlight in one hand, gun
in the other, rousing the city boy
from innocent sleep; awake
he was guilty of a whistle,
a touch in the palm of a
white woman's hand
they charged.

He was fourteen and he was fresh
as clean laundry.
His mother considered the ruins
of her once-beautiful son.
The hanging eye, the missing other.
The tongue cut out and hanging.
The privates pried off.
The head hacked, front
from back.

How articulate was this wrecked flesh!
The remains of her boy, once beautiful.
Then ruined.
She left the casket open.

People waited in a line that curved
around the corners of heartbreak.

Just one glance
and men shivered,
women fainted.
A thousand pages turned, a new place
for the race that had seen enough

carnage of color,
cocky or quiet.

Pendulum

Be careful in journeys through these stark states.
Mountains looming masks of inquisition.

Hooded hills, erect, or flat and deceptive.
The earth opens up beneath you,
The hangman's trap door: you will dangle
And twitch against the landscape.

You know what time it is
By the arc of your body
Striking the hour
This way, then that.

Then, a pendulum
You stop
Held in the grandfather clock
Of the Grand Imperial Wizard.
How bizarre you are!
A grandfather clause of democracy.
A teardrop,
So large,
A log, charred,
A question mark
                    Sleeping in midair.

Night riders crawl under upheld lanterns.
Citizens watch.

They make lariats,
                But will not lasso
                And let go.
They make a noose
                For the moon.
                Bring it down.
                A lone soul
                in perpetual astonishment.

Be careful, Black boy.

                                For Trayvon Martin

Phillis

Every morning a bowl of tears
Lifted to the sun.
This libation shining in a shaft of memory.

Every morning
You would have climbed into the light.

What did you do at night, Phillis
Wherever you slept—at the foot
Of the white girl's bed, in a room
Of your own away from
The clatter of the fat dresses
Of a kind mistress
As mistresses go   and come?
Would you sit in the nimbus of a candle
Reading the leftover lessons
Of sunset
Or writing, writing
Each letter a libation to night,
Every poem
A sleepwalk in a nightmare land?

Did you make angels of New England snow?
And fly away in your mind
On a gently forced rhyme?
Your life anomaly, original.

Your skin a perfect pitch singing inside
Pressed against cumbersome dress.

Your tongue longing a lullaby
Like a leaf that skimmed the terror
From the top of the ocean you crossed.

You said the sufficient truth you could
In language you pruned that pruned you.
Your pen overflowed with gratitude for the redemption
Of Christian slavery that washed your soul whiter than
Freshly fallen New England snow.

Were you the first to write whose memory they stole?

Recalling only the gesture in early morning—
Libation lifted to the sun.
Your fragile frame
Cut off from any love save this tainted gift.
Then your arrogant, Black husband, you kissed him
Like the ground of Africa, didn't you
Take him early one morning
To meet your mother
And lifting your libation of songs up
He whispered in your hair, "Woman,
That is the sun!"

After Work

After this comes bliss,
that's what you told Tedium and blooming Impatiens.
Or maybe it is now at the door, the beggar
with a hand full of sunlight and a mouth full of thanks.

After all
this is a place where blood sugar drops, and water rises
to meet the occasion of a troubled hope.
You would be standing on a porch after canning
the best preserves of your girlhood
in clean glass jars, placing them in a dark
hard room below ground
and looking off down a worn road
to a place where sun settles down.

But
before that moment you opened the door
and only noticed the little wind,
small as a child's breath, brushing past you
into your living room, or wind rustling
at windowsills like tiny elegant kittens,
delicate, limber, and innocent.

Now
you're on that stark wooden porch
standing and staring down the day
you worked so hard on.

Your body is dressed and stained
with all your cunning canning.
Your fingertips and palms purplish
then blue as everything you've loved
inside yourself.

Soon
you'll give up the road,
and the promises trembling in the dusk.

You'll say the hell with it, or
the heaven, or the earth,
turn around and walk back into your house,
your stained dress, your sweat sizzling.

And the beggar will have found work,
will be Home, a natural man,
a rough and tumble angel,
sitting at your table, hands washed,
mouth smiling one story after another
beaming like the sweet
you drowned your best fruit in
so something of a girl would keep.

Then
you go into your hard
dark room and bring up a cool jar
to twist the top off and say,
"You may use your fingers."
And you do.
And he does too.

Vocabulary

For Marion "Tumbleweed" Lett Beach

In those days "bitch" was a word
that grown folks used like a spare
tire when the regular tire went flat.
It added height to an argument;
it preceded the elevation of fists
to blows. "Bastard" was its accompaniment.

Godmother said, "I called that man
a jackass. That's why he kicked me
in my butt. He put his hands on me
twice, grabbed my wrist. 'Come on.
Let's you and me have some fun.'
I wouldn't go. 'Take your hands off
me, you jerk, you jackass,' I said
when he wouldn't. He
kicked me in the butt when I
tried to get away on the ice.
He was kicking me. The men
on the corner said, 'Schoolgirl,
is that your husband?'
'I've never seen him before
in my life,' I cried. This
was unusual. Stuff like that
didn't often happen. They let me
back in the drugstore where
I worked. He was angry because
I'd called him a jackass.

Nowadays everybody's angry.
Be careful what you say to these
people in the street."

It might come back to you in a shot.

\\\

It is not Lake Michigan's lapping waves
Dun-colored without glow . . .
—LANGSTON HUGHES

the Red Line Is the Soul Train

For Marcel Townsel

1

This is the El in the middle
of the expressway, dividing
to and fro; looking up from it
old houses still stand guard.
I see the people who know
all the ways of the weather
and ways to heat—
oil, coal, electricity—
even the sun they could turn on
when they claim their power.

Now I am cold and without my power
on the El they call the Soul Train,
where people sell anything you can buy:
cassette tapes, gloves, candy, hats, socks,
cigarette lighters, wallets.
You can even sell your soul to Jesus
for a dollar and get a pack of M&Ms
or a bag of peanuts.

Before this train there was a valley
filled with concrete, and before that
a field of rabbits, clay, and grass,
and before that half a neighborhood;

it hurts to remember bliss of wholeness
where now remains serfs and bloody
turf.

Remember shops and stores we went in
and out. Once crossing the street alone
at six for a grape bubble gum I barely missed
being hit by a car. I can feel the fender
pressing air against my running body.

You always have to wait for the Soul Train
to take you somewhere, then take you home.
The Train of Souls somber or amused
by sights and sounds. Conversations
that conclude with strangers no longer
strangers but riders like you on the Red Line
where a quick nap is a whisper of heaven.

In winter you can take your gloves off.
You don't have to fight
the cold.

2

Uncle James named Jim, Mama, Aint Emma, and them
played burying the dead, shouting and speaking in tongues.
Mama, beautiful as a sacred film star, wailed,
"Oh, my boy!" for her ether-child whose birth and death
ecstasy-merged with young, jerking limbs
as she thrashed before her grief grew strong as her body,
who knew what was in store for her to lose?
What doubled her over, bent her back, and swept her
off her feet and threw her, was too heavy for Uncle James
named Jim or Aint Emma and them other child-
church members to bring back into the fold.

So they gave up precocious bereavement, gave up
the life-sized Holy Ghost what got my mother
the girl who hurt too much to play redeeming
and release from sorrow which hadn't found her
yet was on its way. All this happened
back through the blood-line.

3

In the time before this time everybody is
unemployed or one-tenth of everybody, I
was at loose ends, having untied myself
from one purgatory into another.
Watching a talk show, I heard a man say,
"I made myself happy," with tiny tasks
when he was unemployed and working
in the library to bide his time.

So I decided to make myself happy and sang
while in the hostile places doing diminished work
about the joy the world didn't give to me
and the joy was in the song ripping through the air
like a pair of play scissors cutting sorrow.
I told the mean-eyed woman what I never knew
I knew, "Life gathers meaning as you live it."
I hadn't yet fallen into the pit they'd dug for me,
only circled and circled around it.

4

My godson came to visit, a godsend,
"You been praying with an attitude," he said.
"You walk up to God and holler up in His face.

You grab Him by the collar and say
You better give me what I want."
I confessed my truculent prayer,
the posture of a gangster or a thug.
"Pray with humility," he said.
"Just say Father, the way Jesus did.
He'll hear you."

So I started with a cup of syllables
that I had forgotten about
and began to brew another lifetime
of words to drink.

The British like their cup of tea to save sanity.
Me? I steep a pot of poems to carry me
through the frigid territories of the years
I left behind but go ahead of
into the crowd. A cup of syllables,
an intimate peace I pour for each of us,
a magic shivering in a saucer,
a light arising like smoke,
so clear it clears your head of the cold
that's going around.

For all these many, many years I've been
chipping ice, melting it. It had gathered around
me, smothering my life. So I've been working
on my own behalf. I'm like a child playing church
or a woman in one. Simply another soul
riding the Soul Train. Sitting here with
my gloves off. Waiting for God to smile on me.

Home. I steep my pot of poems, blood-red prayers,
a strengthening to pass along the Red Line:
Love, Peace, and Soul
Power.

Notes above the Stream a part of the Stream

In Water Tower Place there is a waterfall
That flows down the center of a stairwell,
A little stream of consciousness.
Every now and then a bubble of water
lifts up, hangs in the air, and bursts.
Its individual beauty, rounded like a note,
Stunning, then falls
back
into the flow.

Rosa/ rose so.
Her education in her hands with light inside them.
She sat and sewed a straight seam,
a road to follow as we flowed a thousandfold
while empty buses rumbled emptily on wicked wheels.

Fannie/ ascended
Stopped time, trembled, her testifying sweat
under the hot lights of a television sun.
"I'm sick and tired
of being sick
and tired." Hands working the land like light, water.
She fell back into the flow. Splashed
and kept on going.
Rosa/ rose
"I'd like to be remembered
as a person who wanted to be free

and a person who wanted
other people to be free."
Free/ a little stream of consciousness
flowing out of memory into history.
Each one/ rising.

Notice the notes of water
as they spring up, resilient, leap up a cry for justice,
fall back into the stream of this commercial place,
a clear consciousness,
continuous, vivid, splendid.

Each one of us/ rising
on a moment's note.
Shining, hanging round in air,
trembling and falling back
into
a fluid descent of striving, and decent dissent.

A Woman Was Being Raped

on an El platform. Just about daybreak
on a weekday when the first commuters were on their way to work.
She was screaming, her mouth stretched wide as the river she was
drowning in. In mid-rape a train going by stopped for the stop.
The people on the train were amazed and pointed out the couple
fucking on the El platform this time of the morning. The man
is a man, they said, but the woman must be a dog. Look at that bitch—
somebody get a water hose, someone clever said, hose 'em down,
and she hollerin it's so good. Others tittered at the sight of public sex,
her skirt askew, coat thrown open, spread, blouse torn down to the bra,
breast tumbled out, his zipper unzipped, privates private in her
underneath the ragged scream she screamed, wild turbulence,
the doors closed on the sounds she made. The train kept on its way,
blue fire licking out little tongues on the sides. The first commuters
on their way to work heard it on the radio, between the time
they punched the time clock in and out. The memory of her kept them
awake throughout the day.

Do you remember her face? Would you know her if you saw her?
Did she look like me?

Eclipse

We carry the news with us. It sits in the eyes
Like cold tears, like the lake at midnight
And the dark thick and cold we say we see through
As we study the company of stars in the North American sky.
It comes to us like this:
Miami, in the state of bloody flowers,
a Blackman gunned down by a silver badge on an immigrant policeman
From an island stolen from a blue Caribbean sea.

By the Great Lake whose name's meaning is long lost to us,
On the landfill, in the frozen-breath dead of winter,
From the stone steps of the observatory,
We witness the eclipse,
The round, pearl-faced moon in the shifting sprawl of clouds.

(I wonder if once someone divinely human read clouds like tea-leaves
in this same dark blue cup of sky.) Now
we are artless here, unskilled laborers lost under leaves of cloud-
gathered cold. We blow into our hands. Our fingers too stiff,
too betrayed to pull a trigger. Our sight too poor, too blind.
Is this how far we've come by faith?

The cup runs over in a perfect curve across the moon, over and over,
Until all that is left is a silver worm of light,
or a single-celled animal.
The rest is obscured by a quick flow of cloud, moon behind shadow,
Shadow behind clouds.
We blow into our hands and say and pray that we evolve.

lu

SUITE: IDA

Not myself nor my reputation,
but the life of my people.

—IDA B. WELLS-BARNETT

Ida Watches

Eternal vigilance is the price of liberty.
—IDA B. WELLS-BARNETT

Who goes there? shuddering in the night wind,
bones knocking tinnily like venetian blinds
in a window. I look out, a watch woman
over history, a race woman. I loved you
and hid you against thundering hooves
and white wicked wizardry. I called your names
out one by one to be counted like stars or teeth
knocked out or buried in the deep blue mouth of a land
that should have been a heaven.

After riots in Elaine I visited sons in the executioner's
cells. "Quit talking about dying." I paraphrase myself—
"An Almighty God has the power to set you free.
Pray to live and believe you are
going to get out." And God

opened the doors and sons walked
free as a Negro could be in a land
that was supposed to be heaven but
was not.

Still I am the watch woman watching
what I would rather not see. The executioner's cells
in the eyes of our own. The blood sport spilling.
I must say the Time of Our Sorrow and the Time
of Our Tomorrow on the brink of Despair
or Jubilee if we pray for it and believe.

two trains

The countryside slides away, bleeds trees,
sunlight rolls down like a savior.
The train shudders and hisses to a stop.
Which train?
Who is in the wrong spot?

A seat on a train is the site of a war.
Ask Gandhi, East Indian in South Africa;
Ask me, a colored school marm, in skirts, hat, and gloves.

We lost the battle, and won a war.
Equally colored.

There is something about insult that burns
bodily as one is seized and dispatched
like an angry letter full of inkblots of significance.

Gandhi led his story.
I wrote mine,
in my way led by matchlight.

Did Ida B. Wells Ever Pass Bessie Smith on the Boulevard?

Blood gushing from her arm like water from a fire hydrant,
She lay on the side of the road under the pale hands
Of a white doctor who stopped to tend her on his way
To go fishing. She shivered and twisted in pain. He
Decided not to wait for an ambulance and stretched her
Out in his car. Mississippi moonlight shone down on them.

Ida, on the other hand, died in an apartment on a boulevard
Not far from here. What blues poised on a turntable
On the boulevard of the living kept her awake so long?
Scandalous music, race just the same. The souls
Kicked up the dust and summoned the sight of ghosts
Of everything that would be: blood gushing from a torn arm,
blues raining from her body. Bessie. Her civilized cry
"Send me to the 'lectric chair," set right with Ida B.
Who only half-listened to such because it was anti-lynching,
Involved due process. "Here's a woman I could like!"
What would the club women say but "give me a pigfoot
And a bottle of beer" then claim respectability and close
The door on you. Hard. Like the hit of that car that
Crashed into Bessie and the doctor on the way to the
Hospital. A final violence.

Kokomo

(Mississippi, 2000)

And you would unfold
And look at the map
And think "Whoever

Heard of Kokomo?" Fold your map.
Then look out the window of just
Washed years
At landscapes and man
Shapes dangling like grotesque leaves

You have come to see. You were alive
When Billie
Holiday wrote "Strange Fruit"
and sang it. Her voice lonesome as a train
In the middle of the night.
It is broad
Daylight.
Wide as sunshine,
Uncontained.

Then you snatch up your valise,
And leap off the train,
Press down your hat,
Hitch up your skirts, and
Race to witness the remains of a boy

Beloved by a bevy of girls white
And black with faces like stained
Glass, the *Pietà*, you have seen it
Before

The stretched out man-boy stretched
Across the lap of a death-bedazzled
Black Madonna

And you will unfold your map
And look for the year of where you are
And only a few will remember
Will know who you were

As you step over puddles of blood
Of a Black boy
And who he might have become
Past Kokomo.

V

The wind and the rain transforming
my house to an island, a bare rock
in the sea . . .

—DENISE LEVERTOV

Looking Back

If I say this is our last look at the island
Then maybe it will be true
And we'll look and not be salt
But like the moon removed from it
In a territory of our own, moving away.
We were not Robinson Crusoes who arrived
Shipwrecked, but kidnapped from a land
Of the sun, coming by canoe, contrivance,
In the deception of deepest night.
Looking one way it will seem like
Bikini Island wearing a vast mushroom hat
Or a Puerto Rican isle being tested under protest.
Its flowers and trees stalked,
Ruined for all time or only a century
Or two. Looking another way it will be Haiti
With her Ton Ton Macutes who move in a whisper,
Spiriting away rebellion, or Elmina, Goree, a window,
The startled stumbled steps, the row of rooms,
The door cut out of the dark, open
To the sea that has no doors, no way
Back, every eye a window into weeping—
A look at deceit, then the unknown,
Heartbreak, or not, the sea has no music,
Only a gasp. At last we will be stolen treasure
And we will call it Treasure Island and
We'll have dug until we found ourselves,
Then leave the rest behind.

Betrayal

In another life woven out of Obatala's cloth of excellent character
You sold me for beads that laughed back at African sunlight and shone.
My children you gave to Goree, to Elmina.
And you knew what it was you gave me to—
You fed me as succulent meat, satisfying flesh
To a bitter beast endlessly greedy to solve his appetites.

We were not all innocents, even though your skin is the same as my skin.
Then in the increase of centuries of acquisition—
You grew in numbers, swelled.
We are not all innocent now, although you drape yourself in kente cloth
And barter with the bitterest of beasts.
Your heart like his a well-oiled machine.
It gives away humanity, magnificence.

I remember how you helped them at Middle Passage.

Hot Pink Flamingoes

(September 1997)

The tiny zoo in which elegant flamingoes
Hot pink and obedient, marched
In drill formation, could not
Occupy my concentration that wandered

Always back in memory to another island
When I was not alone, over forty,
And convalescing; wondered but
Did not brood like a hen nestling eggs

That would crack open from the inside,
And a bright yellow chicken burst
Through, her tiny beak open in a cheap
Cry. Memory is a presence, a consolation,

And a puzzle, constant and amorphous. I
Wondered where so much of life had
Gone and how to grab another September
In my two hands and hold it until
I got someplace with someone I wanted

To be with, until I knew some of
The answers to some of the questions
I didn't know then to ask. I had
A sip or two of spirits with a strange

Man named Joe whose story was his wife
Had left him with no notice; he came home

To a cleaned out house. I laughed something
Like, "What did you do to her?" He wouldn't
Say, but said she reeled off a montage of charges
Against him. He would have liked a hotel romance
With a stranger with no past-due complaints

Or strange ones. Like me. "Go home. Talk
To your wife," I said or words to that effect.
"You must still love her." About me, he said,
"He doesn't love you the way you are."
How could he have known? You loved me
On another island, another time, when there
Were no pink flamingoes, only a rooster
That crowed to wake us up throughout the day.

Fuchsia

On the boat she reclined
In a fuchsia bathing suit.
While he sat
And watched her.
Enticing creature that she was.
Mellow from being
Out of the bottomless water,
In love with him.

Quick-limbed,
He made fun of her,
Fearing the deep, cold ocean.
She flapped her wings
Like a chicken
And squawked.

She was right to have been so afraid.
Think of the years they spent
Wandering, plowing
Through deep water.
Losing sight of each other,
Seeing, now and then,
A bobbing head.

the scarf

Infants you must take care with—
The soft spot in the middle of the head.
Hold them just so
Like cupping a priceless vase;
The mouth open to contain mysteries,
The grains of remains of a loved ancestor.

Some women, some men, you must take care
With. We are so easily misled.
It's the soft spot in the middle of the head.
Dreamers, give us a hint, a subtlety,
A half-spoken promise.
All this, sufficient to weave a bliss
That floats out of that soft spot
In the middle of the head.

Believe me. I will never change.
I will always be a baby who smiles
During a dream. My skull tender as a veil.
A scrim between one world and another.
Now I will float a dream like a question
In a comic book, and hope a hand to hold it
Firm, and work hard, an honest heart.

Believe me. I know the difference now
Between ignorance and bliss.
A dream grows up and protects the soft
Spot in the middle of the head.

A lie dies and longs to live
But there is nothing it has to give.

All this knowing comes from having been misled
Before I began wearing all day and to bed
A scrutinizing scarf
Over the soft spot in the middle of my heart
And another over my head.

the Rape of Memory

I could not remember what I never knew.
And still cannot.
Because I did not know
What they thought I knew
And never intended I should know

To make my story mystery to me
To rob me of sights so that I could not see
To rob me of sound so that I could not hear
To rob me of smell so that I could not detect their stink
To rob me of taste to remove my grace
To rob me of touch so that I could not feel as a woman.
The physical basis of memory
They removed.
Meticulous and specific
To the senses.

The connection back and forth
Between us
Is the physical basis of memory.

Their grand design
To interrupt the sign language of love,
To make my story mystery.

I don't know what will happen to me
When I am truly old
And all the years swiped and wiped
Are smooth and blank as ice.

We have not approached the answer of forgiveness.

Sleep

I know the names and bodies of certain trees—
catalpa with its monkey cigars, white-barked birch, tree of heaven that stinks
on high.

I know the shape of my nephew's back going down the alley. I know who
he is not.

I earned an education; books opened their spines to me, spread their leaves and
spoke in seductive whispers.

I recognize blue jays, cardinals, parrots, red-winged blackbirds dipping
in the sky,
raucous crows, and corporate pigeons that stain the sidewalks of concrete
divided by the cracks
I do not step on lest I break my mother's back which does not break.

I've known spiders, clever and kind, or malevolent.

I learned manners—to say "please," "thank you," and "you are welcome," even
when you are not. To open doors and hold them open for others
to follow through.
I learned to defer.

I clothed my nakedness.

I wash dishes when I have to and dust when I must. I am still inside when I do
duties.

I know the meaning of money.

I learned the shadow-side of good people, the worse side of bad people.

I have heard voices.

I am myself and someone else yet to be.

I know the names of too many movie stars and too few heavenly bodies.

I burped no babies that were my own, only borrowed for hungry joy.

I traveled back to Africa and to islands in between. I was a tourist in a grand dream.

I gained and lost my weight in gold.

I sat at windows, waiting for my story to unfold down the avenue,
like an intelligent spirit ahead of me.

I walked on blackberries fallen free on the street of memory,
on walnuts in coats in the park near the dark lagoon where the brave geese
dwell.

I've watched wars on television, seen floods and the sodden aftermath of floods.

I watched Love hide his face from me.

I heard rumors, inklings.

If I should die before I wake
I'll miss what it occurs to me
did not occur to me.

VI

All about are cold places,
all about are the pushmen and jeopardy, theft . . .
—GWENDOLYN BROOKS

American Justice

No one has told you that it hurts to be bound and gagged
Like Bobby Seale in the courtroom of the once Chicago Eight
Then Chicago Seven. And I am very much a woman.
I sing because I am not free. I sing because I hurt
to be bound so long you have forgotten who I am
And who I used to be and what I stand for. I ask you,
"Are you surprised by what you see in a lopsided land?"
I couldn't say.

"I may be twenty-six—but I'm an old woman in disguise,"
Aretha said then and she was right. So I'm singing to you
From the heart
Till the door closes on me and a dream of a man
Encased in a bubble above my head like lines
Of conversation in a comic strip.

I ask you, "Are you surprised by what you see in a lopsided land?"
I will sing for you as when I
Was twenty-five a thousand bound years
Ago.

There's a reason why Aretha drives her voice like a car,
A pink Cadillac, with the top down. Close your eyes and see
A star over a dusty city. Outlines of lives filled in smoke,
Concrete. And you cruise through decades, and feel
Unbound, with the top rolled down. There's a history
Hidden in Aretha's voice. The quick river we crossed,
The turbulence in the air, the Freedom Riders riding,
The fire next time, out of a South of children hungry

Dancing before a shotgun shack singing, "Look in my eyes,
What do you see? Surprise. Surprise. You just like me."
I see more than that.
In all shades. But I couldn't say; that's how they paid me
For speaking up.

And my voice flew away from me on its own, then came back
Wiser to me. I remembered how Nat Turner lay down
In a field and saw visions as a gift from God alone. And
I knew what love was and is and loss going down slowly.

Grace is a gift I can never see. It comes to us threaded
Through the eye of a needle. I am a poor woman.
I am queen of my soul.
I sing because God made me.
And I sing because I am not free.

Applause travels
Like rain and may pass over me.
But my song comes back
Home to sit in my own chest
After I pour it on you like sunshine
Or sorrow you already know
Traveling like Mercies to console you.

I can put it on you
Till you start to mumbling your troubles;
Eyes surprised to see what you see in a lopsided land.
When I sing like an old woman
With a flowing spring in her voice.
A healing touch.

I'll know you understand
When you take my trembling, trembling hand.
And it is still.

In these Times

I have lived so long with trouble in mind. I long for those days we drank
Joe Louis milk, when we bought it where we could get it. Ate tea biscuits
not too sweet but delicate, delicious from Mama's hands. A happy childhood
is a space to walk inside on bare feet. As we age we long to become again
dancers of the current and ancient dances in the original dream. Remember
how we dreamed in drums outlawed long ago? Echoing from our heart beats
contraband, inaudible across the bitter distances. It is why love must be
discreet or the crows will gather and pour their harshened songs into the air.
I have lived so long with trouble in mind in these astonishing times. I need.
I need to know the song of my story opened out of mystery and sorrow
so I can sing, and dance indiscreet without missing a true heart beat
yours or mine.

Warm Weather

Hold back spring!
Hold back summer!
Hold the unfair weather
That brings

Showers of lead
Criss-crossing
In streets.

Here comes the green!
Here come the leaves
Sprouting suddenly
On trees.

Here comes Death
Come out to play.
To take children
Home tonight, today.

Must be for money,
Grudge, or greed
Or envy
Or spite against God.

Death comes out to play.
To take our sons and daughters away.

Beginner's Luck

1

I was a lucky girl,
    unfurled like a flower
in a safe garden, locked
by love from trespass
and trampling. So sweet
the memories, the perfume of years.
The life of each of us
is too brief;
we are lucky
to have had
any of what we had
that is not punishment
or tempering
for an unknown reason.
Our hope that someone
will love us
and lock the gates
to keep us safe
for all our days
while inside us
Luck is unfurling,
opening us
to a long-lived life.

2

I had so many aunts, and so many uncles.
And one mother and one father.
So many sisters and two brothers. In-laws.
And a plethora of cousins. Nieces and nephews now
grand or great ones.
Grandparents. I remember on both sides
of Time.
My mother's father would put one hand
in his pants pocket, touching money he would give
us for solving his riddle.

Such long, wide sight of memory.
Sometimes I've had friends.
I was destined to be happy.
To have all that I have.
A thousand cowrie shells rattling
in my pockets.

3

I haven't always had what I wanted
and I've wanted what I could not have.
But I have a holding heart
that keeps people inside. I am
a lucky woman.
A thousand cowrie shells rattling
in my pockets. I was destined
to be happy in this moment.
In this immeasurable moment.

4

A while ago I was singing
about my happiness;
now I know my summer-student is gone,
not much more than twenty-one.
He was killed at a party,
a case of mistaken identity.
He was unlucky, wasn't he?
And the burn of it singes my tongue.

In every cowrie shell
there is a serrated howl
in the pockets of many hearts.

5

Someone opened a gate, trespassed, trampled.

6

We are, each, a cowrie shell rattling in God's pocket.
What is Luck?
Who can solve this riddle?
Who can do it in a minute?

7

He was lucky then. A culinary artist,
he had a gift. His words danced.
I remembered him. He was so vividly drawn.

His words danced irrepressibly, rattling
on the page in an act of divination.

His luck ran out.
But a part of him stays inside
rattling in us,
keeping me awake this night.

Nocturnal

Nocturnal: he sleeps
All day, flying through
Stumbling dreams.

In high school he dreamt
Of all the daring things
He would do, given
Half a chance.

Places he would go
In his own ride.

Day washes over him
Like all the admonitions.

At dusk,
He rises, rolls his sleeves up,
Tests his guns.

He lets his pants slide down
Past his hips.
Goes down and under
His old junk car
His only need, his only hope.
His crouching life.

Niger: No Exit

A child, a brown child
brown skin with ragged pink open sores,
lying still, so still.
Not even twitching to the tiny touch of flies.
Another with parasites in her mouth. O, Africa!
Could not eat
if there were something.
Still, so still.
Others eat thin rodents,
Rotting carcasses
of cattle.
Flies everywhere.
Flies lighting, rising, lighting
on the drought-dusty faces of children.
What would weeping do?
Still I do.

Years before a little brown girl
put her head on her desk
and cried out
she wanted nothing to do
with Africa.
"They got flies all around they heads!"
she said.

Years before, I was not much more
than a brown girl
in a pristine classroom.

We read Sartre's *No Exit* or
Was it *The Flies*?
Flies everywhere.
A metaphor for hell.
I don't believe in hell.
Only heaven God ostensibly forgot,
yet keeps circling around
lighting, rising, lightning
on the surface of the world,
the faces of children.

VII

I still smell the foam of the sea they
made me cross.
—NANCY MOREJON

the Last Door

(For the survivors of Hurricane Katrina, 2005)

In Goree
The Last Door
a threshold, a hole
a doorway cut in stone
in time

one side African
the next   unfree

slave

American apartheid
one sign   White
the other   unfree

Colored

All our days colored
with the bitter erasure
of our names

the half-erased
discolorings of our competence,
our selves

the second seat
or the last

The Last Door, out of fetid, dank darkness
out of the flood

seeping under
into our shabby shoes

until we walk
a ragged step
like people in shackles

but walk
where there is no way,

on water,
filthy though it be,

unfree and
free.

Glory Land

*(In memory of the Africans of Jamestown, and
for my mother, Angeline, who named me.)*

Angelo they wrote, a man's name
And named me the same, man's name
out of ignorance or spite or haste or casual hate,
a flourished *o* instead of an *a*
for Angela.
Both of us deprived; I paid
to have my name made right.
Mississippi Bureau of Records.
She was forgotten as "Negro Woman"
night-woman spilled out of Treasurer, a treasure
assigned for servitude, at the pleasure
of Captain William Pierce and wife, June.
Each day pierced her heart, Negro woman.

Mareo, Christian, Nando, Acquero,
Palmeno, Cuba, Salvo, Angelo, a man's
name for a woman. Slave. Treasure.
Names engraved on a gallery wall
at Jamestown, Virginia, where Africans came
on a ship seized by pirates from pirates
of human matter and mist of dream.

Angela pounding grain in Angola,
land of cassava, ambling cattle, craftsmen crafting
with stern, nimble fingers, miners of rock salt
and tar, makers of shell money
not human money.

Christian Angela who wrote her own name,
literate and lovely. Angela captured on a beach
in Luanda. Ship set sail to crucifixion
piercing her heart. The last look at her home's land.

Do Lord, oh do Lord, oh, do remember me.

Wash, dust, chop, scrub, rub, cook
in the captain's house.
Counted in a census as Angelo
a Negro woman, seeing her
but not seeing her.

Dark Angela, a shadow to them.
Who came out of Africa, by way of Treasurer,
treasure, my namesake
forgotten.
I am a servant like she
who once drank from a cup of custom
and memory.

        I, Angela
        Angolan.

        American
        Against my will.
        Before there was
        America.

        Angela.
        Still.
        Stepped out of a ship.
        Into captivity.

Oh, Lordy! Do, Lord.

1661.
Servitude wheeled into slavery
in perpetuity.

> I, once servant.
> Now slave.
> No birth date, no death date for me.
>
> The smell of tobacco in the air.
>
> I am between the ones who were first
> And the ones who stole me.

Now
a President says,
"We are a nation of immigrants."
His memory lapses my kidnap.
This two-faced land
of hope and anguish.
Where we are seen
and not seen.

Angela did not live to see the Paradise land, honey and milk
in every cup.

> Is it true
> you make your own Fate
> like a bed
> you sleep in
> or a dish
> you eat?

My Fate was stolen.
And I must salvage mine.

Do remember me.

Was her name
foisted upon her
like a goose is force-fed
grain to fatten its liver
for foie gras—
she who once spoke
Bantu?

My name is an heirloom,
Angeline, my mother's
great great grandmother enslaved
in cotton, and her Angeline
daughter born 1867—
and my mother's father's sister,
Angeline, my mother, Angeline
reclaimed my name as Angela,
a jewel
reset
in a modern setting,
ancient.
We polished it,
with the cloth of our skin
until it shone.
Passed it on to the niece
and then passed it on.

Imagine the solitude of her days.
The dull clamor of the household.
Did she have any descendants
to venerate her?
To follow their bloodline

back to her to Africa,
vibrant, exuberant, and colonized?

Do Lord, remember me. I've got a home in Glory Land that outshines the sun.

Dusting. Her brown hands slide
over wood cut out of wilderness.
She remembers once memory
skips like black wax over
the terrible journey over water.

The stench. Twice-stolen.
Stolen in mid-sea. The gruel.
Suffering unanimous, bottomless
at bottom where she slept.
Beyond sleep. Vomit. And
sweat. And feces. And urine.
And terror without direction
in the bowels. And who to touch?
Thrown together. Shackled.

Brown hands slide over furniture.
And hover over the glint of memory
of home, fleeting sunlight
flashing through the window.
These hands gripped pestle,
ground grain. Gut sent up a girl's
laughter.
Blink, and there they are—
The African grasses leaning
one way in the wind.

Only female fingerprints to wipe away,
prayer circles, whorls and whorls semi-
erased by rosary beads.
I consider the nunnery,

as novice and physician
in darkest Africa, a missionary
among distant relatives with white smiles
and eager hands receiving me.
Sunlight pours through a dining room window
like wine spilled over the long, heavy table.

I see the isolate specks of dust
on the surfaces, so many dreams,
glinting, such humanity.
I am a detective
with a colorless husband,
who is more than smiles and hands,
inside the double-conscious mysteries,
solving.

Inside the living room
my palm and fingers slide through cloth
over shelves and end tables.
I am dark and holding as shelves and table.
I do not leave my prints.
Here in the convent.

Home. I gaze unblinking before the screen.
Water knocks me down.
So many of me runs a distance,
returns.
Dark force against white water.

I got a home in Glory Land.

A name attached yet
never misspoken as Angelo.
Always Angela.
Angela Yvonne.
A name as utterance, sinewy, feminine power.

The admired Angela.
The sheltered one.
The only one.
Brilliant crest of hair, rippling like grasses
in the wind.
Ubiquitous Angela, hidden in our hearts.
A name not miswritten.
Fairest by degrees.
Elucidating master and slave, each maimed.
Flame. Bright. Destroyer and Purifier.
Seen. Not unseen.
In plain sight.
Escaped.
Exonerated.
Lifted up.
And out of anonymity, Angela
a Negro woman, lifted thus.
African, ancestress angel.

Do, Lord. Oh, do Lord. Remember me.
Even when I cannot remember.

Particulars of her life and mine
wiped away. Lost.

I do not know the details
of the stories that have touched mine,
rubbed me wrong and caressed in solace
and affirmation like a coin
I am.

I do not know the details
of her lost life,
remembered only as one.
Among twenty
who touched this

land as stolen dream,
broken memory. Fear source. Conscience-burden.
First circumstance from wrong to worse.
First who thirsted while others sipped.
And hungered while others supped on their morsels.
Firsts in Jamestown, Virginia—
out of these shadows
a nation sprang.

Do remember me.

What is a name but sensible and sacred?
Utterance
attached to brain, limbs, heart and gut.
Spine and eyes. Ears. Nose. Mouth.
Hands. Feet. Soles. Souls.

Wholly human Angels. Black and glorious.
Angela or not-named Angela
but the same as she:
African and American.

She steps out of the shadowy veil
at last
to be seen.

I got a home in Glory Land that outshines the sun.
I got a home in Glory Land that outshines the sun.
I got a home in Glory Land that outshines the sun.
Look away
beyond the blue horizon.

Haiti, It Has Been Thirty Years Since I Last Saw You

Haiti, it has been thirty years
since I last saw you.

An island set upon so much blue
water,
so many kinds of blues.

Haiti, I remember you.
I was a tourist in your heart,
a witness to the ache.
I loved the beauty you created
of wood, iron, and bright paint.
Haiti, it has been thirty years
since I last saw you.

In the morning I was waited on
by silent servers. I ate calm yellow eggs
and toast tinged by the taste
of charcoal.

In the afternoon I languished
prettily in a pool of dreams
away from the asking eyes and outstretched
palms.

One day winding through the high mountains
we passed a silent funeral procession on the side

of the road that winded us in surprise; strangers
we mourned momentarily,
below the smell of vetiver in the fields.
Perfume an improbability.

Now older and nearly numbed by funerals
of ones I loved and knew, I pass through
my days silent against sorrow except for the surges
of grief that seize me.
I have heard the news of relentless
powerful hurricanes that savaged you,
and the cruel self-slavery
of your children that was
beneath you.

Yet I am not your daughter.
Once I feared I would drown
in the heavy water
off your coast.
I had no idea that your sorrow
would go on
as the island itself erodes
losing trees to charcoal,
I can taste still
in the morning toast.

The Moment of Arrival

*(In light of the Movement, to the Moment
of Barack Obama as President; for David L.
Crockett-Smith and Vivian Cooke Buckhoye)*

We set out with grim necessities
and sky-tall masts, yet tenuous expectations, unmade maps

wanting to disembark at a new land
imagination dreamed—milk and wild honey,
wide fruit trees, river, fish leaping,

vegetables sprouting; a plenitude pleasing
to the body and soul, we sailed toward,

stopping at many ports along the way,
shopping for staples and spices,
acquiring rich fabrics and trade beads for money,
the art of conversation in many tongues,
repairing for repairs.

We have practiced our "civil rites" in barbarous provinces,
severe climes. We have prevailed against winters of stinginess,
savage, bitter.

At last we broke free into smooth as glass
movement, dancing forth
to this shore of pleasing plenitude.

We disembark and kiss the new ground,
praising our old ancestors, and the Divine
Providence that gave us this trade
of all we left behind, setting forth

in dream-led youth, forty years at sea
through the bitter angers, choosing "better angels"
to be our guides and abide with us
here in a place richer than we imagined,

its dishes seasoned with the sorrow
of all our years, and the laughter of our survival
welcomed bright with each sunrise.

In this place of arrival
the possible is possible.

ᴜᴧᴧ

I dream of the drums
And remember.

—LANGSTON HUGHES

The Smoke Queen

(In memory of W. E. B. DuBois)

I am the Smoke Queen; I am Black.
Now you see me. Now you won't.
Stand back. The fire rages.
The blacker the berry the stronger the juice.

I am the Smoke Queen; I am Black.
Now you see me. Now you don't.
I hover in the air in the castles of Elmina and Goree.
I trembled above the waters of Middle Passage.
I troubled the waters where I leapt
To be free.

I am the Smoke Queen; I am Black.
I am the memory of myself
As I stood silent on the auction block,
Separated from my body
As smoke while they counted the number of my teeth.
In my own tongue I shushed my child.
I said, "Oh, baby, don't you weep."

Those who measure me find me lacking
What it means to be human, wise.
They count the number of my teeth;

They weigh my tears on the cold scales.
Yet
I am magnificent, rolling like thunder over houses.

I am the Smoke Queen. I am Black.
Now you see me. Now you don't.
Now you see me. Now you won't.

I stoked the furnaces of factories; I wrote
My love letters on a train with a wisp of
Myself guiding me home.
I am the Smoke Queen and. I am Black.
Hungry in the stairwells of public housing,
A private power beating in each heart.

I am the Black Smoke Queen. I am Black.
There are no gray areas except those I sweeten
With my hush and my mercy.
How many centuries have I waited above
The water my soul to reclaim
Wade, wade in the water
My soul to reclaim.
Oh, I am the Smoke Queen. I am Black.
Now you see me, now you don't.
Look for me in the whirlwind.
Garvey's ghost and Nzingha's regality.
The throbbing hum of Simone's song.
Now you see me. Now you dare not look.

I believe in the substance of each soul.
I believe in the clean cloth of character
And reputation earned, deserved.
I observe who you are and what you do.
I lift you up on smoky arms.
Where there is smoke, there is purification,
Ritual.
I am the smoke above the campfires
Where we rest on our way.
I am the smoke above sustenance and comfort,
Signaling.

I am the Smoke Queen. I am Black.
Now you see me. Now you don't.
Now you see me. Now you won't.

I am the X that marks the spot
Of the lynch rope still hot
And the body charred.
Myself a cry I sent up over the remains,
Lingering, hallowing, in your nostrils
And the chambers of your heart.

I am the Smoke Queen and I am Black.
Out of humiliation, I lifted my own spirit.
I did not look to the hills.
I looked to the horizon. I go there.
Sensitive to the winds of time and wounds
Of toil
I caress your skin.

Light as the spirit of flight
I fly to you
I caress your soul
Who you show and do not show
The world.
Here, there, elusive to all who tried to catch me
Before I was holy, live
And dancing over my own head.
Higher!
I am the Smoke Queen. I am Black.
Now you see me. Now you don't.
Now you see me. Now you won't.

I turn on myself, churning, turning in a whorl,
Shape-shifting in the winds of history.

I am voices rising out of eloquent earth,
Resonant with ages, fertile and sensible.

I am chief citizen of the room
Where blues presides.

I rise with the steps, intelligent and eager,
Of old and young hurrying to know a cloud
Of mysteries.

Of truth crushed to the earth and rising
Rising, again and again.

I am the incense that heralds the presence
Of the holy.

I am the Smoke Queen. I am Black.
Now you see me. Now you don't.
Now you see me. Now you won't.
Now you see me. Now you don't.
I am the Smoke Queen.
I am Black.

the Good Neighbor Observes the Celebrity Next Door

If you going to do something you ought to go on
And do it right instead of making it up as you go
Or turning out something need to be turned back in.
It ain't so pretty what they flocking to gawk at like
Geese, everybody going one way with one expression
On twenty faces. If you going to accept that type
Of applause with two hands squeezed into fists to fit
The praise in, you got to take the criticism too.

I was hanging intimacies on my line looking over at her
Goings on. My briefs so bright they knock your eyeballs
Back to white to go with my whites just to look at them.
It was the sun give me a squint. It was the sun.
Who that lying say she saw water and a wipe on the sly?
I-Have-A-Allergy. I told you that before all this bally-hoo
Over her Creation of Creation. When I find me some time
Behind this line, and this soap, and this water, and these
Swole hands I will present my Revelation. Then everybody
Will know who is who.

I been working on something. Oh, this old rag, this little
Number, it's old, nothing of interest, didn't nobody notice
I been had it on off and on for weeks. But everybody ain't
No Big Dipper in a small well.

Though I wonder why and why not sometimes when I look up.
All that blue and them stars winking at me I want to pluck

Them out. Like this gray hair come out of nowhere to
Meddle me and make me old. The Bible say if your eye
Offend thee pluck it out. The same rule apply to the rest
Of the body. Every body but hers. She think she escaped.
But I got news for her: the Bible is a heavy book.
And it can smash the best of them.

You Do Not Know the Hour

You don't know the hour—
Old women and ministers of every faith
Say (then look content at the prospect
Of Death's clever descent through any window
Locked or not. The unexpected
Guest who makes himself welcome, even
When we don't want him.
Sweet milk disappears from the standing
Glass. A cough turns into nothing.
Blood slips out the corner of the mouth
To meet him. We soil ourselves.)

You don't know when the hour
You'll be sitting on a couch, a chair,
Or stool and look down and over
At the pile of dirty laundry; the light
Walking at an evening pace through the window
From the next room catches a piece of everything
And you, even—the tip of your shoe—and you
Know then what is good.

                The sweet milk is in the cup.
You can cough and bite your tongue
And taste blood. For one second we are
Each clean. And no one has hurt anybody.
Including you. And if you wanted to imagine Death
You couldn't. It doesn't matter.

Heaven Is No Recompense

Who ever you love you will lose
Sooner or later. Even you.
And you will grieve for who
Ever is lost. Even you.
How can you lose unless you hold?
And how can you hold without
Touching, being touched.
Each stroke a stroke of luck.
Pity us. And love the luck.

For Gwen, On Her Passing

Your legible voice is gone from us.
And lost newspapers spin and whirl in black and white and fly
And slam against lampposts—blood
Red all over.

Who can remember a time when your language
Did not dignify what or who was diminished?
In the end you lived in a world where they put poets in boxes
Or cages where they could watch us in the killing-zoo.

The sorrow is this—you did not live to see us free.
Certain eyes are too old for tears.
What could we have said? Or what would we have said
If we could?

There is none like you that we love a whit as much.
You were yourself and no one else.
You gave me few particular gifts,
But each of these I kept. What is mine and mine alone.

I will not squander
The light that runs
Through my hands
When I hold your poems.
Yet
How empty my hands feel
When I try to write about you!

I am no match for you.
And never said I was.
I stretched my spine, strengthened.

But your words were mother's milk—
Oblique, expressed, nutrient.
The steady, exquisite throb
Coursed toward our heart's muscle,
Understated as a pulse
Pulsing into pictures taken deep inside
The chambers where we weep.

Whoever begrudged you respect or honor?
I almost curtseyed before you once or twice.

But the years,
All of them, a fleeting glance,
I so rarely saw you, waved from a distance; wave.
You wave back and go on.

the poem in the pocket

For Serene Foulks

My younger sister loved a gifted young poet
who was my friend. They made a daughter
seven months before he died at twenty-five.
I wrote a poem about these lovely and sad
events.

One bright day three or four years later
I rushed home from reading poetry
and placed a folder full of my poems
on a chair while I performed a chore.

My four nieces, toddlers, or not much more in age,
that daughter among them, fell upon the poems
and threw them about like miraculous white leaves
all over the floor.

I returned. Chastising the mischievous girls,
I gathered up the poems. All but one
I could not find.

I made the gifted poet's daughter
clutching her pocket,
let me see what was inside.

There I found the poem about her father
carefully folded
and hidden in her pocket.
She who could not yet make sense of alphabet.

I knew there was a poet in this event.

It was not me.

Faith II

Is it by instinct we light
In pews like monarchs
Come home to sleep and dream?
We flutter,
Eyelids,
Other than that quiver of belief
In a still presence,
We take to the air,
In search of what?
But here
We always forget.
Rub wings softly
Spirituals,

Salt of the earth and air
And make a wish,
An ineluctable prayer.

An African Reunion

> My grandmother crossed Atlantic River
> in 1821.
> —MARY MARIAH JEFFERSON JACKSON
> 1885–1984

My heart learned the language of empire,
learned who I was not; a sorrow-self
that did not melt like a wafer
in the mouth, but made a song
that would not be pressed down;
soared, jagged, and searched
its way out into open, pressed against
stained glass windows and lingered as a wish.

A girl's soul searching the ways and gestures
of a people forgotten.
My life searching through thoroughfares and
backward glances, sibilant asides, and
secondhand accoutrements of a courtesan land.
I studied in universities of a new and jaded empire
stumbling upon ancestral ways,
and learned the name of Shango. One night
in a nightgown dancing inside against the rain
and running from window to window shouting
Shango, a learned name, I met a clap of thunder
so loud I flew from the glass like a bird
startled by a lion.

Then to live a life forgetting
and trying to remember, searching
for a sign.

One middle summer of an empire at war
in the midst of a great, predicted storm
on an interrupted walk I had braved anyway,
I sat silent in a bus kiosk and watched rain pour
and lightning rip through the sky,
a burning spear directed toward the city.
Shango casting down bolts
and thunder applauding behind.

The heartbreaking city disappearing, dimly
re-created, revealed in the heart's eye
another time, a whole people of many peoples,
green lands, great limbs of trees,
Orishanla broken now sealed anew.

I sat like a schoolgirl in the kiosk,
hands folded in my lap, rain slanting
into my glass and steel sanctuary,
dousing my clothes.
Suddenly, I opened my mouth and sang,
"Shango!" "Shango!" And that song
then redemptive, loud-round as a world,
a wish fulfilled.
More than sign, but wonder.

I walked home in clothes drenched at the hem,
as if I'd skimmed Atlantic River.
Not knowing if it were a river or an ocean,
but close, and cool
as the baptismal pool.

the Ritual Calendar of Yes

Who owns the Time owns the earth.
Opening the ritual
Calendar we celebrated the Yam
Festival, making do with sweet potatoes
Delicious in the Candied Yes.
    We devoured
The First Yam, and filled clay pots with
Shivering animal dreams and blood.
    Danced till Time
Sat in the seat of the town and I sang
The descent into the membranes
    of memory.
Holding midnight and morning, one
    in each
Breast, two swinging round as
    twin earths.

So those seasons barren or plagued
    where you live
You have taken a new god, neglected
    the festivals.

I close the calendar of ritual.
Do not disturb the moment or history.

This night I bless
The gates of the city. Anoint
The four directions of sorrow,

Four rhythms of music
In one voice. Joy is in my eye.
An iron rod would not disturb the
Eyeball of my ecstasy. Nor sizzling fire
Stick remove the song of my arrival. If
This city would die it would stand
Again. Where is the Land Where Death
Meets Life? Here. There is no departing
     the City
of Collision and Levitation.

I am with the Owner of the Time.
     I am One with the Owner
of the Time. Who owns the Time
     owns the sun and the moon
brainbowl and heartsystem.
I am One with the Owner of the Time.

Leaf

The cowrie shell is so tiny you cannot
Hear the song of the Infinite inside each one passing through
A serrated edge of dream.
When we wear them on our bodies
They rattle and keep us awake
So we do not miss anything.

She leans her head back on the couch
And I witness her, a young mother-to-be,
Round with child, her face round too,
Down to her nose. I think then that
I am mortal and will never live to see
Her children's children's generations.
Already
I am a greedy ghost hungry
For the living.

The baby wants to play on his great-grandmother's bed
Where he can eat the Bible, instead of simple paper.
In each dry leaf the taste of Paradise.

To a God who does not barter,
What is there to give?

April 6, 1991

I have traveled through years of remembering, weeping
in spots. Tender to touch the memory of tears that bowed
the cheeks and ran into the mouth like twin rivers into
an ocean, while the rank stream ran snot into an ocean too.

Like an appraiser of gems I have inserted the eyepiece
to scrutinize the authenticity of stones, to weigh the
meaning of some semiprecious injury. How much is this
worth or this or that. What is the value of being
in what way—victim, witness, wanting, angel absorbed
in the ingrown nail of a traveled heart.

Then I saw it, while sitting in the bathroom, on the shut stool,
not expecting to see what was in the middle of me—
the pearl of a smooth orient—red, blue, discreetly washed
into the shimmered skin of herself, a kernel of tight light.
And with its sighting, a UFO in the belly, a shove,
almost contraction, as if a presence ever present were born.

Again, in the morning, on the couch, I asked for it,
what I had been protecting all these years,
and it was a burst pearl of light, leaping in spears, out and
out. This earthquake between navel and womb was all I
knew to say the body eloquent and alive, willing the mouth
to speak for me. So I am telling you what cannot be told

unless you love words and lean into each one as the bruised
mouth of a lover, lips swollen from desire or discovery
so sublime tissue swells, raw and sweet, to convey it.

There is such a place in you. A star, secret and secreted, and
secreted by cells. It is what you protect. You may speak for it,
you may speak for you. You may have words now and not die.
Now your eyes are dark skies that give without running out.
And your mouth most certainly is a prayer book,
each leaf bright with delight, burns, turns so no one can touch
what is within, unless you say.